CHANWAKAN WIN

The Sacred Tree Woman

Jerrie Lea Printup

Gotham Books

30 N Gould St.
Ste. 20820, Sheridan, WY 82801
https://gothambooksinc.com/

Phone: 1 (307) 464-7800

© 2024 *Jerrie Lea Printup*. All rights reserved.

No part of this book may be reproduced, stored in a retrieval system, or transmitted by any means without the written permission of the author.

Published by Gotham Books (December 10, 2024)

ISBN: 979-8-3481-1164-9 (H)
ISBN: 979-8-3481-1162-5 (P)
ISBN: 979-8-3481-1163-2 (E)

Because of the dynamic nature of the Internet, any web addresses or links contained in this book may have changed since publication and may no longer be valid.

The views expressed in this work are solely those of the author and do not necessarily reflect the views of the publisher, and the publisher hereby disclaims any responsibility for them.

Table of Contents

Acknowledgment iv
Preface vi
Dedication Page ix
Introduction xi

Acknowledgment

I would like to begin by expressing my deepest gratitude to my family and ancestors, who have shaped my journey and identity. To my parents, Orsamus Marshall Printup and Ola, for their strength, love, and the rich legacy they passed down to me. My father, an enrolled member of the Tuscarora Nation, and my mother, a descendant of the Cherokee people, embody the rich and complex heritage that has inspired this work.

Special thanks to my siblings—Jeanne, Judy, Jim, Joyce, and Joe—whose companionship throughout my upbringing on the Tuscarora Indian Reserve has left indelible memories. Each of you contributed to the tapestry of our shared experiences and the stories that have led me here. My gratitude also extends to those in the broader Tuscarora and Cherokee communities, whose history, resilience, and cultural continuity have provided me with a deep sense of belonging and purpose.

To all those who have supported me, encouraged my personal growth, and shared wisdom along the way, I thank you. Your influence has shaped this narrative, and I am **forever appreciative.**

Preface

This manuscript is a reflection of the profound and unique journey I have undertaken as a person of both Tuscarora and Cherokee descent. Born into a family deeply rooted in the Haudenosaunee Confederacy, and with the rich stories of the Trail of Tears, wartime service, and cultural perseverance, my life has been shaped by the complex intersections of history, identity, and personal discovery.

Growing up on the Tuscarora Indian Reserve near Niagara Falls, I was surrounded by the vast natural beauty of the land and the traditions of our people. These experiences not only nurtured my connection to the Earth but also informed my understanding of the profound challenges our ancestors faced. The forced relocation of the Tuscarora from North

Carolina, the hardship of the Cherokee on the Trail of Tears, and the enduring strength of my father's service in WWII—these are the threads that weave through my family's story and my own personal narrative.

As I recount my family's history, from the origins of the Tuscarora within the Haudenosaunee Confederacy to the shared experiences with non-native neighbors, this work aims to honor those who came before me and preserve their legacy for future generations. I write to capture the essence of our struggles, triumphs, and the unyielding spirit that continues to guide us today.

This is not merely a recounting of historical facts, but a reflection on the personal moments that defined my upbringing—the simple joys of childhood, the harsh realities of prejudice, and the deep pride in my heritage. It is through these stories that I hope to offer insight into the enduring spirit of our people and the importance of understanding where we come from to know where we are going.

Dedication Page

I dedicate this book to all my courageous "Brothers" and "Sisters" who stood alongside me in the relentless fight for our Native rights. Your strength, unwavering determination, and solidarity have left an indelible mark on my journey, and I am forever grateful for your companionship and support. Special recognition goes to the remarkable individuals who have inspired and empowered me throughout this journey: Jim Printup, Joyce Printup, Clara Moses, Russell Williams, Marty Sheehan, Andy Ligamarri, Alan Davis, Richard Curley, Russell Means, Dennis Banks, Leonard Crowdog, Wallace BlackElk, James Spotted Elk Sr, and Carter Camp. Your wisdom, courage, and dedication have been a beacon of hope and strength.

To these extraordinary warriors, I honor your legacy and the profound impact you have had on my life. Your spirits continue to guide and inspire me every day. A'HO.

Introduction

I was born on February 26, 1953, to Orsamus Marshall Printup and Ola. My father was a member of the Tuscarora Nation of the Haudenosaunee Confederacy, specifically part of the Bear Clan. The Haudenosaunee, often known as the Iroquois

Confederacy, includes the Mohawk, Seneca, Oneida, Cayuga, and Onondaga Nations, and in the 1700s, the Tuscarora joined as the "younger brother" to the Cayuga. Originally from North Carolina, the Tuscarora people endured waves of encroachment, forced migration, and land theft. Many were compelled to journey northward, eventually settling in what is now New York State, where they were embraced by the Haudenosaunee and granted land by the Seneca Nation.

My father, one of thirteen children—only two of whom were girls—was a decorated member of the 82nd Airborne Division. Stationed in Fort Bragg, North Carolina, he met my mother, who had an intriguing heritage herself. My mother's father was a Swedish immigrant, and her mother was a full-blood Cherokee from North Carolina. Although my mother hadn't grown up embracing her Cherokee roots, my father learned about her heritage during a dinner with her family, which led me to eventually trace her lineage to the Cherokee family known as the Tilley's. Like the Tuscarora, the Cherokee were forced from their lands and relocated to Oklahoma on the infamous Trail of Tears.

During WWII, my father made four parachute jumps with the 82nd Airborne before being injured by shrapnel from a landmine. He was honorably discharged and returned to the U.S. to recover, bringing my mother and her two daughters from her first marriage to New York. As he healed, they began a new life together and had more children. I was born seven years after my older brother, Jim, followed by my sister Joyce and, later, my brother Joe. Many years after moving to Kitigan Zibi Anishnabeg Nation in 2001, I also discovered, through DNA testing, that I had an additional brother, Marshall, from my father's time in Hamilton, Ontario.

Growing up on the Tuscarora Reservation, about ten miles from Niagara Falls, New York, was magical. Niagara Falls—one of the Seven Wonders of the World—was a place of great beauty and legend, a story told to us as children about an Indigenous maiden sent over the falls as a ceremonial offering. Our reservation was filled with farmers and open fields, creating an enormous playground for us. I spent my days running through cornfields, climbing trees, and exploring the dense forests full of deer, rabbits, and a multitude of vibrant birds. Life was simple but rich with nature's wonders.

One unforgettable night when I was about six, my brother asked me to help him fetch water from the hand pump outside, about 75 feet from our doorstep. As we made our way, a voice in the darkness warned us to stop—there was a bobcat nearby. I froze, catching sight of the animal's eyes glinting in the light. It was unmistakably a large, wild cat, and before we knew it, a rifle went off. Safely inside, we heard a knock at the door—it was our neighbor who had warned us and scared the animal away. The encounter left us shaken but grateful.

Our home was a modest cabin on the reservation border, a far cry from the cozy log cabins you see in vacation magazines today. It was a compact space with two bedrooms, a small kitchen, and a living room that doubled as a sleeping area for me, my sister Joyce, and my brother Joe. My older brother Jim had a small private space in the attic. In the summers, we often had cousins and neighborhood kids staying over, adding to the lively, bustling atmosphere.

We had an apple tree right outside the cabin, and my brothers delighted in climbing it, hiding, and tossing apples down at my sister and me as we tried to find them. Those playful ambushes taught me resilience and a sense of humor early on. Some of my fondest memories were spent with my dad in the garage, watching him work on engines and build stock cars and go-karts, which ignited in me a lifelong love for mechanics and creativity.

Life on the reservation shaped me. It was a place of tradition, family, and connection to the land. Every moment—from the wide-open fields to the close quarters with my siblings—has stayed with me, a vibrant tapestry of memories that makes up the story of my roots.

His official job was as a Heavy Equipment Operator, a trade he learned while serving in the military. A Heavy Equipment Operator is someone skilled in operating large machinery such as cranes, bulldozers, trucks, and other heavy vehicles. I also looked forward to harvest time in the fall when some of my dad's cousins and nephews— who were close in age to him—would bring me bushel baskets filled with apples, pears, peaches, tomatoes, and whatever else my mom could use for canning. It was a wonderful gift that helped us through the winter. I think the cousins and nephews did this to make me feel special, and it also gave me the chance to watch the canning process. After all, I was going to have to learn it eventually.

Across the road from us lived two non-native families, as the land wasn't part of the reservation. The road running through the area was a main route from Niagara Falls to the next town, which separated our cultures. Their houses were fancy, with indoor plumbing, while my family had to share an outhouse with the neighboring native family. It wasn't the most private setup, but it was "one big happy family." One of the non-native families, the Haseleys, had two teenage boys about the same age as my brother, Jim. The other non-native family, the Wendts, had three daughters—one my age, one my sister Joyce's age, and one my brother Joe's age.

One time, after a few days of rain, a four-foot ditch that ran along the main road by our side of the reservation had filled up. My sister and I decided to go "swimming" in it. Suddenly, we heard Mrs. Haseley's voice shouting, "Get out of the ditch water, you'll get polio!" We were so scared that we ran back into the house. Although we didn't fully understand what polio was, the sound of it was terrifying—and it turned out it was. The disease was a crippling one, and we were later vaccinated for it, as it was more common in the 1950s.

At first, we weren't allowed to interact with the Wendt girls. We would just stand across the road and wave at each other. Eventually, our mothers agreed to let me and my sister sleep over at the Wendt house. We didn't sleep in the house, but had a "camp-out" in their garage, which was exciting since we hadn't done that before. It was also different since we had never experienced indoor plumbing. Another time, we stayed at their grandparents' house next door. It was a large farmhouse, but we slept in a small shack that I think was an old chicken coop. That experience turned out to be scary. We were all lying there talking when we looked out the small window and saw a bouncing fireball, jumping all over the ground. When it came inside the shack, we covered our heads. After that, I never wanted to stay there again at night. To this day, I can't explain what we saw, but I never went back. We stayed friends with the Wendt girls through the years and cherished those memories.

Fridays were exciting for me because Gramma would sometimes buy the family ice cream, which I think was her way of thanking my parents for giving her rides to and from her work at the Niagara Falls Airbase. I'm not sure what she did there, but she walked a good part of the way. My grandfather, a very proud man, did not like accepting "hand-outs" or "sympathy," and he certainly didn't want to rely on others for rides for Gramma, but my parents did it anyway. He was a cross man, likely due to his time at Thomas Indian School, where the government sent Native children away from their families to assimilate them into white society. My grandfather didn't smile much, except when he used his cane to hook someone around the ankle. In 1960, he passed away from cancer. I remember how frightened I was when my parents took us to the funeral home to view him. I thought they had cut off his legs because I could only see half of him in the coffin. The funeral director had to open the casket to show me he still had his legs. A few days later, I saw the hearse go by, and I swear I saw my grandfather sit up in the coffin as though to scare me—and it worked. A couple of years later, Gramma passed away from a stroke, and I missed her dearly. Her piano playing, speaking Tuscarora, her love, the cooking on the wood stove, and the large family gatherings filled with children, grandchildren, and great grandchildren were special.

A couple of years later, we moved into the family homestead. My dad's brothers and sisters decided to let us live there. I imagine he was chosen because he was born in the main part of the house, the day after the addition was completed. I loved being there, reliving my childhood with my grandparents, uncles, aunts, and cousins. My grandparents owned property on each side of the house, as well as behind it, and the house was far from the main road, which provided us with a lot of privacy. I enjoyed planting strawberries and creating gardens with my dad. I would wear a harness and pull a plow to help make the rows for planting. After the harvest, I would learn from my mom how to can the produce.

In 1966, I had my first real "crush" on a boy from a nearby reservation. He went off to Vietnam, and we wrote a few letters before I stopped hearing from him. I thought he had found someone else and got married. I was young and moved on with my life. Later, I found out he had been killed in action. My cousin, who was a sergeant in the Marine battalion, told me he had pulled him from the killing field. I was sad but spent time with friends to stay happy—friends like Marty, who grew up like a brother, cousin Andy, and friends Clara and Bossy from grade school. My sister, Joyce, was always part of the group. As teenagers, we became involved in Native Rights, especially as the Vietnam War raged on, and many cultural movements were taking hold—anti-war protests, the Black Panthers, and the American Indian Movement. We traveled to various Iroquois communities to learn about the language, dances, songs, and ceremonies of the Haudenosaunee people.

In 1969, the Chiefs and Clan Mothers of Tuscarora decided to evict all non-natives from the reservation. These people had lived there when the New York State Power Authority took some of our land to build a reservoir for the Niagara Falls water supply. It was time to reclaim the land. The protest camp we set up across from the trailer park on the border of reservation and non-native land was supported by other

Iroquois territories. By the late summer, tensions escalated into violent confrontations between the protesters and non-natives, with guns drawn on the protesters, including my oldest brother. Eventually, the non-natives were evicted from Tuscarora land.

After the protest, my brother Jim helped us form a group called "Messengers of Everlasting Peace," which aimed to promote pride in our culture and restore our traditional ways of life as Haudenosaunee. We spent the summer working on "The Akwesasne Notes," a Native American newspaper, and became more politically aware of Native rights. The work we did would shape our future involvement with Native causes.

I became increasingly involved in protests and began learning about my Haudenosaunee traditions, particularly the longhouse ceremonies, songs, and dances. I traveled to longhouses in Six Nations, Seneca, Salamanca, Allegany, and Onondaga, where I felt a profound sense of belonging and love. I wanted the same for the Tuscarora people—a Longhouse of our own. Historically, longhouses built in our community had been burned down, mostly because the majority of our people were Christians. I do know, however, that one of my uncles was married in the traditional Longhouse way.

In 1971, my primary goal was to graduate from high school and then dedicate myself to Native rights activism. A group of 10-12 young people raised money to purchase a van for our travels. We had it plated, insured, and my father took care of the repairs to ensure it was roadworthy. Two days after graduation, we set out for the Tonawanda Reservation, where other Native Nations were gathering for a Unity Caravan headed to South Dakota. My father escorted us until we left and headed westward.

As we traveled through various states, we witnessed numerous violations of Native rights—Native women being raped, Native men unjustly arrested or beaten, and the justice system punishing them harshly for minor infractions, while non-Natives received minimal repercussions for far more serious crimes. Our caravan took these complaints seriously, confronting local courts and law enforcement to make it clear that our people would no longer tolerate such mistreatment. There were some physical confrontations between Natives and non-Natives, but we managed to make our point.

The caravan ended at a park with a small lake, possibly man-made. It was a hot summer day, and while people swam, many were cut by broken glass in the water, mainly beer bottles. In response to the injuries, a respected Elder and Medicine Man from the Seneca Nation, Beaman Logan, performed a ceremony. I watched in awe as he walked on the water, not in it, and as lightning struck near his feet. A few of us helped him back to shore, where we discovered that the bottom of his feet had been charred black. We treated his feet with traditional medicine, and he was able to walk away normally. This experience deepened my respect for the power of prayer and traditional healing.

We continued our journey, meeting up with the American Indian Movement (AIM) and the occupiers of Alcatraz Island in South Dakota. Alcatraz had been taken over by a group of Native activists, led by

Mohawk Richard Oakes, in protest after the government returned the island to Native tribes following the closure of a federal prison.

When we reached Rosebud, South Dakota, we traveled to Grass Mountain to meet Leonard Crow Dog, a respected Lakota Medicine Man and AIM supporter. I had joined AIM in 1970, when Russell Means climbed aboard the Mayflower in Boston Harbor as part of a protest. Crow Dog was a spiritual leader whose ancestors included great Lakota figures such as Crazy Horse, Sitting Bull, and Black Elk. I connected with several Alcatraz occupiers, and we discussed the challenges facing our people and strategized future actions. Leonard Crow Dog held a "Name-Giving" ceremony for those who lacked traditional names, a sacred rite before engaging in important actions.

During some free time, my lifelong friend, Clara Ann Moses, and I joined two Alcatraz occupiers, Big John Halleran (Pema) and Delbert Lee (unknown tribe), for a ride on two lassoed horses. It was a nice break, and I missed my own horse, which I had left with my younger brother in New York. As we neared the meeting grounds, we noticed a cabin was on fire, and we helped hold the water hose as the fire truck arrived. It was a difficult task, and I had never realized how hard it was to control a powerful hose. After the fire was extinguished, we returned to the discussions on Native mistreatment. It was painful to hear the devastating stories, as I had experienced racism, but nothing at this level. The experience deepened my belief that we all must respect one another as human beings sharing this earth, without transgressing against one another.

After the meetings, our group made a stop in Chicago, Illinois, where there were complaints about Native girls being raped and Native men being unjustly treated by the justice system. We camped in a local park while the men addressed the issues with the authorities. What started as a "Peace Caravan" often clashed with local law enforcement.

As we made our way back to New York, we needed some relaxation, so we stopped at a Pow Wow in Tama, Iowa. It was a fun time, meeting new people, experiencing different Native customs, and learning new "49er" songs—songs with English lyrics that held powerful meanings for the new movement.

Back in New York, we gathered at my parents' house and helped with the construction of a new furnace room, using traditional dances to assist in the work. We stayed in touch with other Nations about ongoing racial tensions near our Reservation and made plans to support the Onondaga Nation, which was fighting the construction of a major highway through their traditional lands. The Traditional Clan Mothers of Onondaga lined up in front of the heavy machinery, halting the work. I was moved by the power and leadership of the women.

During this time, John Lennon and Yoko Ono visited the Nation. I was so excited to meet them that, while preparing Sassafras tea, I forgot to rinse the roots before boiling them, making the tea appear muddy. Bill Lazore, my "brother" from Onondaga, laughed and teased me, saying, "You can't make mud tea in the Mud House." Bill had been a guide and protector during our "Peace Caravan." He was from Onondaga and made me feel at home with his family. I ended up staying with them and living in Onondaga, especially as the community was waiting for John and Yoko's visit.

One day, while waiting for them, I got impatient and left the Mud House, only to run directly into John Lennon. He put his arm around me and asked where I was going. I replied, "Nowhere," and he escorted me back inside. The group sat with the media, sharing views and discussing issues. I was struck by how down-to-earth they were, not at all like the "superstars" the world saw. John's visit left a lasting mark on my spirit, reminding me that we meet many people in life for different reasons. I am thankful for every person I've encountered along my journey, as they have all helped guide me.

As an eighteen-year-old, I was eager to experience my culture and life. My father was a wise, hardworking man who taught me love, respect, empathy, strength, wisdom, and the importance of love for all. I knew these lessons would help me make good choices, and I hoped they would guide me on my path. After the protest, I stayed in Onondaga and continued learning from those around me. I lived with Bill's mother (the Clan Mother) and his younger sister. Their small home, though modest, was filled with love and warmth. Eventually, I worked at Bill's small grocery store and later took a job at Syracuse University in a Sorority House. It was an educational experience, meeting young women my age, living a different life than my own, yet sharing a common connection in our human experience.

I kept myself occupied with Longhouse ceremonies, activities, and spending time with friends and work, maintaining this routine throughout the spring of 1972. I eventually decided to return to my home in Tuscarora, renting a small house across from my childhood home for a year. By late August, our group traveled to Mohawk Territory in Akwesasne. The publication of *Akwesasne Notes*—a Native publication focused on Native issues—was being handled at Mike Boots' home. We assisted with packaging and mailing, alongside other young Natives from various tribes.

Upon returning to Tuscarora, the men received word from Russell Means of the American Indian Movement (AIM) that a caravan, known as *The Trail of Broken Treaties*, was forming in California to head to the Bureau of Indian Affairs (BIA) in Washington, D.C. The caravan aimed to address a list of grievances: illegal land theft, inadequate healthcare, dishonest leadership, and more. This was amid the ongoing Vietnam War and the Black Panther Movement. In 1968, the American Indian Movement had been founded to combat injustice toward Native peoples, becoming a powerful force throughout the U.S. and Canada. Notably, in 1970-71, the occupation of Alcatraz Island took place, led by Mohawk Richard Oaks and other supporters under the group name *Indians of All Tribes*. My curiosity was piqued, and I wanted to hit the road in support of my people. But I had promised my parents to graduate high school, which I did in June 1971. Just two days after graduation, I left to join the fight for my people. I made an oath to put my life on the line, with no fear—because they were worth every fight.

In April 1972, I learned of the corruption surrounding the Tribal Chairman of the Oglala at Pine Ridge Reservation in South Dakota, which further motivated me to act.

I left Tuscarora on November 1, 1972, to join the protest in Washington, D.C. with my sister Joyce and her partner, Bossy. We were escorted to the Lincoln Memorial for an overnight stay, where the crowd continued to grow in numbers. The next morning, we gathered outside the Bureau of Indian Affairs building to present our grievances to government representatives. Unfortunately, much like other officials, they evaded addressing our concerns—many of them were Native themselves, but more accurately, "sellouts." As tensions rose, we entered the building and searched for documents to support our claims, which we found and confiscated.

At the BIA takeover, a Medicine Man performed a Name Giving ceremony in a large banquet-style room. Wallace "Mad Bear" Anderson, my older cousin and a Medicine Man from my reserve, Tuscarora, encouraged me to get my name translated into Lakota, as I was entering the conflict with AIM. Mad Bear, who was also my father's first cousin, knew I was destined to become an AIM veteran. When I was asked by Leonard, one of the Medicine Men, why I wanted a Traditional name, I explained that I was from Tuscarora and had always sought peace among all people—but would sacrifice my life for my own people. I was smudged and given the name "CHANWAKAN WIN," which translates to "Sacred Tree Woman." I felt a deep sense of pride as I looked at Mad Bear, who smiled widely. In Mohawk, it meant "Mother of All Nations." Mad Bear told me I was destined to be a warrior, and I envisioned the "Tree of Peace," the Haudenosaunee symbol of everlasting peace for all. I could see my loving arms embracing everyone.

After the ceremony, I went up to the second floor of the building, where I found Vietnam veterans holding their "fort." These men, veterans of my era, were those I was proud to know. I thanked them for their service to the country and especially for their support of our people.

As vehicles prepared to leave the BIA building, the cars filled with people heading to different locations. My sister Joyce and her boyfriend, Bossy, left with a Tuscarora friend, while I joined Russell Means and a few Lakota "warriors," heading to North Carolina on a mission. Upon arriving, we were warmly welcomed by the local Native community with a delicious meal of baked fish. Among those with us were Tuscaroras, Lumbees, Cherokees, and other tribes traveling in the caravan. The camaraderie among us was powerful, and I felt safe with my friends, who acted as my bodyguards. We were hosted in a mobile home overnight, with some of the men standing guard over a truck full of important documents, hidden in a deep area dug into the ground.

Around dawn, chaos broke out. The men came running into the mobile home in a panic, telling us to "get out." We fled into the woods for safety, and later, we learned that the FBI had raided the location where the documents were being guarded. The men on duty had been arrested, including my Lakota friend, Dave Chief. He was one of three Lakota friends I had been traveling with—James (Mickey) Spotted Elk and Al Long Soldier, along with Russell Means and other AIM brothers and sisters.

We continued our journey through the southern U.S., heading west toward Oklahoma. The Ponca tribe of the Red Nation had invited us to a victory dance, and we were welcomed into their community with open arms. After a short stay, we resumed our journey to South Dakota, dropping off friends along the way. We visited Pine Ridge to drop off Al Long Soldier, and Dave Chief was still in jail in North Carolina.

James and I then traveled to Rosebud Reservation, where I had been the year before. I knew Leonard Crow Dog and Wallace Black Elk, who had given me my Traditional name at the 1972 BIA takeover.

At Rosebud, we visited Grass Mountain, a small community in the hills along the Little White River, where the Crow Dog family resided. The area was guarded by AIM security, providing a safe haven where AIM members lived in teepees, tents, and houses. Everyone had duties—cooking, cleaning, cutting wood, hunting, gathering medicines, washing clothes, caring for children, and preparing for ceremonies. I stayed with the Crow Dog family in their main house, helping Gramma Crow Dog with cooking, food prep, and dishes. I spent time listening to Grandpa Henry's stories of ancestors and the Lakota ways.

During our stay, James asked Grandpa Crow Dog if we could be married during the upcoming peyote ceremony, so that we could unite before heading into conflict together. When Grandpa gave his approval, James asked me to marry him. Although I was a little shocked, having been traveling with him only a month, I agreed. I called my dad, who reassured me, saying he raised a smart daughter who could make good decisions.

The peyote ceremony was sacred. We sat on the floor close to the earth, as the drum and rattle were passed around and the peyote medicine and tea were shared. Each person could sing sacred songs, or pass the drum and rattle to the next. As the morning star appeared around 4 a.m., the ceremony reached its climax. Leonard Crow Dog and Wallace Black Elk, the Medicine Men, had James and me stand while the Elders performed our marriage ceremony. It was a long process, and I fainted, but James helped me stay upright so the ceremony could continue. Finally, we were married on December 16, 1972.

The following week, I brought James home to my reservation in New York to meet my family. We traveled by bus from Valentine, Nebraska, and I returned to the small house I had rented across from my childhood home. While it was good to be back, the place no longer felt like mine, especially with my sister now living there with her boyfriend. James and I soon left to stay with an elderly woman I had once cared for, spending a cozy Christmas with her and her husband—such kind, caring people. Not long after, James and I decided to head back to Rosebud, South Dakota.

Once back, we joined our "family" of AIM members and lived among the Crow Dog family on Grass Mountain. It was a life rich with tradition, where I learned so much about the Lakota people and their ancient history. I began to pick up their language, as it was essential for communication; for many, it was their first language. Grandpa Crow Dog shared stories of the 1868 Fort Laramie Treaty, through which the U.S., having lost a battle, ceded large areas of land to the Lakota. But soon after, in 1871, the

U.S. reclassified Indian lands, forming the Bureau of Indian Affairs (BIA) to govern them. General Custer's campaign against the Lakota led to his defeat at the Battle of Little Bighorn, but it also sparked the illegal seizure of the sacred Black Hills. Then, with the 1887 Dawes Act, Congress confined the Lakota to reservations, including Pine Ridge for the Oglala.

In 1890, during the "Ghost Dance" ceremonies, many Lakota believed they would be protected from harm by wearing sacred shirts. But tragedy struck with the murder of Sitting Bull and the massacre at Wounded Knee, where Custer's forces slaughtered around 300 Lakota, including women and children. Only a few survived to remember the atrocity, which had stemmed from the Lakota's refusal to surrender their land. Later, in 1932, Congress passed the Indian Reorganization Act, using BIA councils to further control tribes and often encouraging sellouts within the communities.

In February 1973, the Oglala people on Pine Ridge sought to impeach Richard Wilson, the tribal chairman, who then requested U.S. Marshals and FBI support to maintain his position. The Oglala invited AIM to liberate Wounded Knee, the site of the 1890 massacre, from U.S. control. On February 26, my 20th birthday, we celebrated at Crow Dog Paradise. Late that night, a caravan of us set off, arriving at Pine Ridge in the early hours of February 27. We occupied the Gildersleeve Trading Post and then made our way to a nearby church, setting up stations. I converted a back room into a medic office, others organized a kitchen in the basement, and the men constructed bunkers around the church.

By February 28, U.S. Marshals and FBI had surrounded the area with armored personnel carriers (APCs). Our AIM members set up a meager defense with what little firepower we had, and shooting soon erupted. Support from the Oglala community outside was evident, as people rallied in solidarity. Over the following days, the situation intensified, with more Marshals and FBI arriving, and even senators visiting to negotiate. By March 2, sporadic gunfire was ongoing, and a nighttime air drop brought crucial supplies. Richard Wilson escalated tensions by threatening an armed assault, while sporadic violence erupted around Pine Ridge, including an AIM member's house being firebombed.

Each day brought new challenges. As tensions grew, a Grand Jury in Sioux Falls began investigating our actions. Sporadic gunfire and snowstorms continued, but morale was strengthened by demonstrations of support across the country. March 22 saw the revival of the Ghost Dance within Wounded Knee—a powerful and symbolic act. Days later, fuel ran out at the Catholic church, and the APCs moved closer, while we established the Wounded Knee Legal Defense/Offense Committee to address our needs for food and medicine.

Throughout March, government roadblocks and negotiations continued. Despite our limited resources, we maintained a strong front. The night of April 1, government forces denied entry to new medical teams, denying us crucial aid. We subsisted on one meal a day of cornmeal, and as hope dwindled, more supporters managed to hike into Wounded Knee, raising our spirits. Yet, the APCs kept advancing.

In early April, the Independent Oglala Nation leaders attempted to negotiate, even sending representatives to Washington, D.C., but talks failed within days. On April 9, new FBI-backed roadblocks appeared, and shootings resumed. We celebrated the birth of a child within Wounded Knee and witnessed a wedding, but the violence continued. A sniper shot at us one night, and on April 16, an attempted food drop had us fearing chemical warfare until we realized it was simply flour bags that had burst open.

Amid the unending gunfire, blizzards, and arrests, several AIM men were wounded. I helped Leonard Crow Dog treat one man with a gunshot wound between his thumb and forefinger, packing his hand with sacred mud. Another, Milo Goins, suffered a bullet wound to his thigh, and we had to extract the bullet using whatever resources we had. Leonard Crow Dog, a medicine man and negotiator, returned from Washington and hiked back into Wounded Knee, bringing much-needed strength and wisdom.

Through all these trials, we held onto our beliefs, traditions, and unity, seeking justice not only for ourselves but for all oppressed people who, like us, strive for dignity, freedom, and peace. Intense firefights persisted as Frank Clearwater was wounded and transported to Rapid City, South Dakota, where he tragically passed. Vigilante roadblocks resumed, engaging in fierce battles with U.S. Marshals, marking the most severe exchange of gunfire yet, extending late into the night. On April

27, 1973, clashes continued through the morning and into mid-afternoon, claiming the life of AIM member Buddy Lamont—a tragic day marked by yet another loss. Following this, negotiations began in Wounded Knee, seemingly triggered by the heavy toll of recent casualties. The next day, the Gildersleeve Trading Post was destroyed by fire, and Oglala Chiefs joined us at Wounded Knee to discuss the ongoing negotiations.

On May 1, 1973, Buddy Lamont's mother, Agnes, came to Wounded Knee to arrange his funeral. Simultaneously, government officials arrived in Pine Ridge, while Frank Clearwater was laid to rest at Crow Dog's Paradise in Rosebud, South Dakota. Talks between the Chiefs, Independent Oglala Nation representatives, and government officials lasted two days. Buddy Lamont's wake took place in Porcupine, South Dakota, on May 4, with his funeral held the following day in Wounded Knee—a somber day for us all. Adding to the heartbreak, Buddy, a

Vietnam War veteran, had been shot in the back, a painful disgrace to our country.

By May 8, deeply affected by Buddy's murder, I left Wounded Knee with James, along with half of the people there. About 150 remained, laying down arms as the evacuation began. United States Marshals transported everyone to Rapid City, where we were processed and arraigned in court. Around May 17, meetings commenced in Kyle, South Dakota, involving Oglala leaders and White House representatives, with additional talks set for May 30.

James and I hitchhiked to Rosebud, South Dakota, reaching Crow Dog's under the watch of armed guards. To my surprise, my brother Jim was among them. After reuniting, I reconnected with friends and family, cherishing the warmth of community life and aiding Grampa and Gramma Crow Dog. Leonard announced a Yuwepi ceremony, and as night fell, I marveled at the flickering red lights that I believed to be spirits—until we were interrupted by Spotted Elk, who crashed through our barricade in a stolen police car, intoxicated. His disruptive behavior reminded me of why I'd chosen to distance myself from alcohol.

As my pregnancy progressed, I returned to St. Francis, where I found work. Yet, tensions rose when James, who'd been drinking, confronted me aggressively. His grandparents intervened, shielding me from his anger. I soon left, returning to Tuscarora, New York, where I found solace in my home and my son. Months later, James reappeared briefly, only to leave us once more. My son, James Jr., or "Iron Chest," became my world and source of strength.

Life continued, marked by both struggles and triumphs. My son excelled in sports, and I managed work, studies, and motherhood with support from family. As the years passed, I reconnected with my community and joined peaceful protests advocating for the young. However, hostilities escalated, and confrontations led to my arrest for "inciting a riot."

Reflecting on our collective history, I was reminded of the resilience and dignity inherent in forgiveness and faith.

On July 11, 1990, another resistance emerged in Kanesatake, also known as Oka, over a land dispute between the Haudenosaunee people and the local residents of Oka. The Mohawk, with roots dating back to their resettlement in the 1600s from the Hudson River Valley, continued to face challenges to their lands and rights. This resistance carried echoes of our past struggles, a reminder of the enduring quest for justice, respect, and peace.

I have quietly devoted myself to community work in Kitigan Zibi Anishnabe, engaging in actions to raise awareness of issues affecting the Anishnabe people. Among my efforts, I helped slow traffic and distribute informational flyers on the critical issue of Missing and Murdered Indigenous Women. We have two young Nish girls here, and their safety is always on my mind.

In March 2013, I welcomed a group of Cree youth from Whapmagoostui, Quebec, who were walking from Thunder Bay to Ottawa. These young people, led by 18- year-old David Kawapit, had already walked 1,600 kilometers as part of *The Journey of Nishiyuu*, meaning "The Journey of the People." David said they were walking for everyone, explaining, "We're helping ourselves, we are helping our families, we are giving hope to whoever is listening. It gives us inspiration and courage to keep going." They were on their way to Victoria Island in Ottawa for a welcoming ceremony before meeting with Justin Trudeau.

I visited Victoria Island in December 2012 to support former Chief Theresa Spence of Attawapiskat First Nation, who had begun a hunger strike to bring attention to the severe living conditions in her community. Attawapiskat was facing a housing crisis with 24 families living in tents or sheds without running water and 122 other families in unsafe, condemned homes. Theresa's hunger strike lasted until January 24, 2013. She stayed in a teepee on the island, consuming only medicinal tea and fish broth.

Although security at her camp was strict, I was granted a brief visit as a veteran of Wounded Knee '73, though my story seemed to leave little impression on the guards.

In recent years, I've often reflected on the journeys I've taken, from the Oka Crisis to the gatherings and marches here in Quebec. I remain dedicated to the release of Leonard Peltier, who has unjustly served 46 years in federal prison for the murder of two FBI agents—an unproven conviction that used him as a scapegoat. I also continue to support the "Water is Life" movement. As always, if the Creator calls me to act, I am ready to stand up for my people in any way necessary. A'ho.

Myrna and I doing laundry at the wounded.

The picture of a teepee ceremony dated about March 22, 1973.

This is my husband Spotted Elk and myself in front of the church in Wounded Knee (March 2,1973).

The Spotted Elk Family 1973

The group photo specifying the last day of Wounded knee 1973 Final picture. Would be that if my husband, myself, and our Wounded Knee Son.

www.ingramcontent.com/pod-product-compliance
Lightning Source LLC
LaVergne TN
LVHW022233080526
838199LV00123B/623/J